1

THE THESPIAN'S BUCKET LIST

1001 Stagey Things To Do Before Kicking The Bucket

STACY KARYN

For all the thespians out there –

May you all challenge each other to become the best versions of your theatrical selves.

WHERE

you can find stuff

How To Use This Book

This book has been created especially and exclusively for the theatre lovers of the world. Although "thespian" is often a term reserved for stage actors, for the purposes of this book, we're embracing it to describe everyone who is a theatre actor, professional, designer, educator, director, manager, dancer, carpenter, artist, musician, therapist, dramaturg, coach, usher, critic, producer, stagehand, entrepreneur, dreamer, fan, or general enthusiast.

Once this book is in your hands, it's yours to personalize. You'll find lots of blank spaces sprinkled throughout, which will allow you to make this bucket list your own.

So get out there and get doing! Use color, add stickers, turn this book into something you're proud of. And then show it off to all of your thespian friends!

And if you want to document and share your accomplishments, you can always join our social communities. Or, you can tag your photos with #theatrebucketlist on social media.

Just go to www.stacykaryn.com/the-thespians-bucket-list to find out how you can connect. You'll also find some free printable DIY bucket list pages, along with a few other fun freebies you can play around with.

Have so much fun out there!

Stacy Karyn

TRAVELING

for theatre

NYC

theatre hotspots

- [ ] 1. Catch a show at Don't Tell Mama.
- [ ] 2. See the caricatures at Sardi's Restaurant.
- [ ] 3. Go to Shakespeare in the Park.
- [ ] 4. Eat at Ellen's Stardust Diner. *
- [ ] 5. Dine at Joe Allen. *
- [ ] 6. Pay a visit to One Shubert Alley. *
- [ ] 7. See a show at BAM Harvey Theater.
- [ ] 8. See a show at Lincoln Center.
- [ ] 9. See a Broadway show.
- [ ] 10. See an Off-Broadway show.
- [ ] 11. See an Off-Off Broadway show.
- [ ] 12. Check out Feinstein's/54 Below.
- [ ] 13. Go to Radio City Music Hall.
- [ ] 14. Sing showtunes at Marie's Crisis.
- [ ] 15. Visit the Gershwin Theatre.
- [ ] 16. Visit Times Square.
- [ ] 17. Walk down the Playwrights' Sidewalk.

See pg. 95

Write about your favorite NYC theatre experiences here:

USA

must-see theatre

Visit the Following:

☐ 18. California: Medieval Times, Buena Park

☐ 19. California: The Magic Castle, Los Angeles (exclusive)

☐ 20. California: Pageant of the Masters, Laguna Beach

☐ 21. Connecticut: Bushnell Performing Arts Center, Hartford

☐ 22. Florida: Broward Center, Fort Lauderdale

☐ 23. Florida: Adrienne Arsht Center, Miami

☐ 24. Georgia: The Fox Theatre, Atlanta

☐ 25. Illinois: The Chicago Theatre, Chicago

☐ 26. Kansas: New Theatre & Restaurant, Overland Park

☐ 27. Kentucky: The Kentucky Center, Louisville

☐ 28. Maryland: Hippodrome Theatre, Baltimore

- [ ] 29. Minnesota: Orpheum Theatre, Minneapolis
- [ ] 30. New Jersey: New Jersey Performing Arts Center, Newark
- [ ] 31. North Carolina: Belk Theater at Blumenthal, Charlotte
- [ ] 32. North Carolina: Durham Performing Arts Center
- [ ] 33. Ohio: Ohio Theatre, Columbus
- [ ] 34. Ohio: Playhouse Square, Cleveland
- [ ] 35. Pennsylvania: Sight & Sound Theatres, Ronks
- [ ] 36. Tennessee: Tennessee Theatre, Knoxville
- [ ] 37. Utah: Hale Centre Theatre, Sandy
- [ ] 38. Washington, D.C.: Ford's Theatre
- [ ] 39. Wisconsin: Fireside Dinner Theatre, Fort Atkinson

ASIA

must-see theatre

Experience the Following:

- [ ] 40. Cambodia: Lakhon Bassac (opera)
- [ ] 41. China: Xiqu (opera)
- [ ] 42. India: Kathakali (classical dance)
- [ ] 43. India: Prithvi Theatre, Mumbai
- [ ] 44. Indonesia: Wayang (puppet theatre)
- [ ] 45. Japan: Bunraku (puppet theatre)
- [ ] 46. Japan: Butoh (dance theatre)
- [ ] 47. Japan: Kabuki at Kabukiza Theater
- [ ] 48. Japan: National Noh Theatre
- [ ] 49. Malaysia: Kuala Lumpur Performing Arts Centre
- [ ] 50. Singapore: Esplanade - Theatres on the Bay
- [ ] 51. Thailand: Sala Chalermkrung Royal Theatre

THE LONDON

theatre scene

Experience the Following:

- [ ] 52. A West End Show
- [ ] 53. The Royal Opera House
- [ ] 54. The Theatre Café
- [ ] 55. Shakespeare's Globe
- [ ] 56. Her Majesty's Theatre
- [ ] 57. Lyceum Theatre
- [ ] 58. National Theatre
- [ ] 59. Palace Theatre
- [ ] 60. Prince Edward Theatre
- [ ] 61. Prince of Wales Theatre
- [ ] 62. Sondheim Theatre

EUROPEAN

theatre

Visit the Following:

☐ 63. Austria: Vienna State Opera, Vienna

☐ 64. Czech Republic: National Theatre, Prague

☐ 65. England: The Minack Theatre, Cornwall

☐ 66. England: Holy Trinity Church, Warwickshire *

☐ 67. England: Shakespeare's Schoolroom, Warwickshire

☐ 68. England: Shakespeare's Grave, Warwickshire

☐ 69. England: Royal Shakespeare Company, Warwickshire

☐ 70. France: La Comédie Française, Paris

☐ 71. France: Palais Garnier, Paris

☐ 72. Germany: Friedrichstadt-Palast, Berlin

☐ 73. Germany: Semperoper, Dresden

☐ 74. Germany: Theater des Westens, Berlin

☐ 75. Greece: Odeon of Herodes Atticus, Athens

☐ 76. Ireland: Cork Opera House, Cork

☐ 77. Italy: Juliet's House, Verona

*See pg. 95

- [ ] 78. Italy: La Scala Opera House, Milan
- [ ] 79. Italy: Massimo Theater, Palermo
- [ ] 80. Italy: Teatro Antico di Taormina, Taormina
- [ ] 81. Italy: Teatro di San Carlo, Naples
- [ ] 82. Italy: Teatro La Fenice, Venice
- [ ] 83. Italy: Olympic Theater, Vicenza
- [ ] 84. Malta: Teatru Manoel, Valetta
- [ ] 85. Norway: Nationaltheatret, Oslo
- [ ] 86. Poland: National Theatre, Warsaw
- [ ] 87. Spain: Palau de la Música Catalana, Barcelona
- [ ] 88. Spain: National Theatre of Catalonia, Barcelona
- [ ] 89. Spain: Gran Teatre del Liceu, Barcelona
- [ ] 90. Spain: Teatro Real, Madrid
- [ ] 91. Sweden: The Royal Dramatic Theatre, Stockholm
- [ ] 92. The Netherlands: AFAS Circustheater, Den Haag
- [ ] 93. The Netherlands: Royal Theater Carré, Amsterdam

OTHER

cities and countries

Visit the Following:

- [ ] 94. Argentina: Teatro Colón, Buenos Aires
- [ ] 95. Australia: State Theatre, Sydney
- [ ] 96. Australia: Sydney Opera House, Sydney
- [ ] 97. Brazil: Amazon Theatre, Manaus
- [ ] 98. Brazil: Municipal Theater of Rio, Rio de Janeiro
- [ ] 99. Brazil: Municipal Theatre of São Paulo, São Paulo
- [ ] 100. Brazil: Teatro Renault, São Paulo
- [ ] 101. Brazil: São Pedro Theatre, Porto Alegre
- [ ] 102. Canada: Four Seasons Centre, Toronto
- [ ] 103. Canada: King's Wharf Theatre, Penetanguishene
- [ ] 104. Canada: Princess of Wales Theatre, Toronto
- [ ] 105. Canada: Royal Alexandra Theatre, Toronto
- [ ] 106. Canada: Meridian Hall, Toronto
- [ ] 107. Canada: Elgin & Winter Garden Theater, Toronto
- [ ] 108. Chili: Municipal Theatre of Santiago, Santiago

- [ ] 109. Colombia: Teatro Colón Bogotá, Bogotá
- [ ] 110. Egypt: Cairo Opera House, Cairo
- [ ] 111. Mexico: Palacio de Bellas Artes, Mexico City
- [ ] 112. Mexico: Teatro de la Ciudad, Mexico City
- [ ] 113. Mexico: Diana Theatre, Guadalajara
- [ ] 114. Mexico: Teatro Metropólitan, Mexico City
- [ ] 115. Russia: Alexandrinsky Theatre, Saint Petersburg
- [ ] 116. Russia: Mariinsky Theatre, Saint Petersburg
- [ ] 117. Russia: Moscow Art Theatre, Moscow
- [ ] 118. Russia: Novosibirsk Theater of Opera and Ballet
- [ ] 119. Russia: Bolshoi Theatre, Moscow
- [ ] 120. South Africa: Baxter Theatre Centre, Cape Town
- [ ] 121. South Africa: Joburg Theatre, Johannesburg
- [ ] 122. South Africa: South African State Theatre, Pretoria
- [ ] 123. Turkey: Cemil Topuzlu Open-Air Theatre, Istanbul

THEATRE
festivals

Attend the Following:

☐ 124. Bregenz Festival: Bregenz, Austria

☐ 125. Edinburgh Festival Fringe: Edinburgh, Scotland

☐ 126. Oregon Shakespeare Festival: Ashland, Oregon, USA

☐ 127. Shaw Festival: Niagara-on-the-Lake, Ontario, Canada

☐ 128. Stratford Festival: Stratford, Ontario, Canada

☐ 129. Insert Your Own: _____

☐ 130. Insert Your Own: _____

☐ 131. Insert Your Own: _____

Have you been to even more theatre festivals? List them here:

DISNEY
magic

Catch a Performance at...

☐ 132. Disneyland California
☐ 133. Disneyland Paris
☐ 134. Hong Kong Disneyland
☐ 135. Shanghai Disneyland
☐ 136. Tokyo Disney Resort
☐ 137. Walt Disney World

Have a Disney park character sign their autograph for you:

THESPIAN
lifestyle

JUST
for fun

Do the Following:

- [ ] 138. Create a musical-themed playlist.
- [ ] 139. Get an autograph from a theatre star.
- [ ] 140. Go to a cast party.
- [ ] 141. Go to a *Rocky Horror Picture Show* screening.
- [ ] 142. Go to a Renaissance faire.
- [ ] 143. Host a musical movie marathon.
- [ ] 144. Make finger puppets.
- [ ] 145. Participate in a flash mob.
- [ ] 146. Put on a puppet show.
- [ ] 147. See a play or musical at least three times.
- [ ] 148. See a touring Broadway show.
- [ ] 149. Throw a musical-themed party.

THEATRE
lifestyle

Do the Following:

- [ ] 150. Audition for a show.
- [ ] 151. Belt out show tunes in a car.
- [ ] 152. Buy a Playbill binder.
- [ ] 153. Collect more than ten Playbills.
- [ ] 154. Cry while listening to a cast recording.
- [ ] 155. Cry while watching a show.
- [ ] 156. Get a callback.
- [ ] 157. Get paid to do a show.
- [ ] 158. Get rejected.
- [ ] 159. Give a standing ovation.
- [ ] 160. Give a theatre-related name to a pet.
- [ ] 161. Go to the theatre twice in one day.

Do the Following:

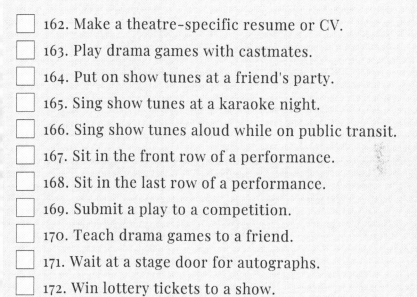

162. Make a theatre-specific resume or CV.

163. Play drama games with castmates.

164. Put on show tunes at a friend's party.

165. Sing show tunes at a karaoke night.

166. Sing show tunes aloud while on public transit.

167. Sit in the front row of a performance.

168. Sit in the last row of a performance.

169. Submit a play to a competition.

170. Teach drama games to a friend.

171. Wait at a stage door for autographs.

172. Win lottery tickets to a show.

Paste your front or last-row ticket stub here as extra proof!

"There are no small parts, only small actors."

— Konstantin Stanislavski

ACT OUT

the following onstage:

- [ ] 173. Crying
- [ ] 174. Sleeping
- [ ] 175. Death
- [ ] 176. Eating
- [ ] 177. Fighting
- [ ] 178. Flying
- [ ] 179. Hugging
- [ ] 180. Laughter

What are the weirdest things you've ever done on stage?

BE A JACK

or JILL of all trades

- [ ] 181. Create a costume.
- [ ] 182. Create a prop.
- [ ] 183. Direct a show.
- [ ] 184. Help build or paint a set.
- [ ] 185. Help design a set.
- [ ] 186. Help repair a costume.
- [ ] 187. Help with strike.
- [ ] 188. Lead a theatre-related workshop.
- [ ] 189. Learn how to play an instrument.
- [ ] 190. Produce a show.
- [ ] 191. Work as a stage manager.
- [ ] 192. Work as an usher.
- [ ] 193. Work at a theatre festival.
- [ ] 194. Write a musical.
- [ ] 195. Write a play.

STRETCH

your range

Do the Following:

- [ ] 196. Be an understudy.
- [ ] 197. Get professional headshots taken.
- [ ] 198. Make an audience laugh.
- [ ] 199. Perform at a Disney park.
- [ ] 200. Perform at a festival.
- [ ] 201. Perform in a musical.
- [ ] 202. Perform in a Shakespeare play.
- [ ] 203. Perform in a staged reading.
- [ ] 204. Perform in an accent other than your own.

What accents have you learned (or attempted to learn)?

☐ 205. Perform in an opera.

☐ 206. Play a character of a different age.

☐ 207. Play a character of a different gender.

☐ 208. Play the lead in a musical.

☐ 209. Play the lead in a play.

☐ 210. Play a villain.

☐ 211. Land a dream role: _

☐ 212. Land a dream role: _

☐ 213. Land a dream role: _

What other unique roles have you played?

EXPERIENCE

the following:

- [ ] 214. A flash mob
- [ ] 215. A musical in a foreign language
- [ ] 216. A play in a foreign language
- [ ] 217. A gender-swapped production
- [ ] 218. A puppet show
- [ ] 219. A show that's longer than five hours
- [ ] 220. A show that's shorter than ten minutes
- [ ] 221. An improv show
- [ ] 222. Ballet theatre
- [ ] 223. Children's theatre
- [ ] 224. Dinner theatre
- [ ] 225. Immersive theatre

"All the world's a stage..."

— William Shakespeare
(As You Like It)

EXPERIENCE

these types of stages:

- [ ] 226. A black box theatre
- [ ] 227. A non-traditional theatre space
- [ ] 228. A proscenium stage
- [ ] 229. A school auditorium
- [ ] 230. A theatre in the round
- [ ] 231. A thrust stage
- [ ] 232. A traverse stage
- [ ] 233. An open-air theatre

List the weirdest places you have experienced theatre:

LEARN
by doing

- [ ] 234. Attend a theatre workshop.
- [ ] 235. Get a theatre-related undergraduate degree.
- [ ] 236. Get a theatre-related graduate degree.
- [ ] 237. Go to a theatre conference or convention.
- [ ] 238. Hire a performance coach.
- [ ] 239. Listen to a theatre-related podcast.
- [ ] 240. Take a playwriting class.
- [ ] 241. Take a theatre-related online course.
- [ ] 242. Take an acting class.
- [ ] 243. Take an improv class.
- [ ] 244. Watch a theatre-related TED Talk.

List your favorite theatre-related TED Talks here:

Get Fancy

- [ ] 245. Attend the Olivier Awards.
- [ ] 246. Attend the Tony Awards.
- [ ] 247. Be a part of a Broadway show.
- [ ] 248. Be a part of a West End show.
- [ ] 249. Be on an original cast recording.
- [ ] 250. Get a standing ovation.
- [ ] 251. Get interviewed.
- [ ] 252. Get mentioned (full name) in a newspaper.
- [ ] 253. Give a speech.
- [ ] 254. Win a theatre-related award.

Insert a clipping of your feature, award, or interview here!

GIVE BACK

☐ 255. Buy theatre tickets for someone.

☐ 256. Donate money to a theatre company.

☐ 257. Help someone learn their lines.

☐ 258. Help with a theatre fundraising event.

☐ 259. See a friend's show.

☐ 260. Volunteer at a theatre or festival.

List some other ways you've given back to the theatre world:

PLAYS

to read

READ THESE

Pulitzer-Prize winning plays:

☐ 261. *Cost of Living*, by Martyna Majok (2018)

☐ 262. *Sweat*, by Lynn Nottage (2017)

☐ 263. *Hamilton*, by Lin-Manuel Miranda (2016)

☐ 264. *Between Riverside and Crazy*, Stephen Adly Guirgis (2015)

☐ 265. *The Flick*, by Annie Baker (2014)

☐ 266. *Disgraced*, by Ayad Akhtar (2013)

☐ 267. *Water by the Spoonful*, by Quiara Alegría Hudes (2012)

☐ 268. *Clybourne Park*, by Bruce Norris (2011)

☐ 269. *Next to Normal*, by Tom Kitt and Brian Yorkey (2010)

☐ 270. *Ruined*, by Lynn Nottage (2009)

☐ 271. *August: Osage County*, by Tracy Letts (2008)

☐ 272. *Rabbit Hole*, by David Lindsay-Abaire (2007)

☐ 273. *Doubt*, by John Patrick Shanley (2005)

☐ 274. *I Am My Own Wife*, by Doug Wright (2004)

☐ 275. *Anna in the Tropics*, by Nilo Cruz (2003)

☐ 276. *Topdog/Underdog*, by Suzan-Lori Parks (2002)

☐ 277. *Proof*, by David Auburn (2001)

* Give yourself a star for each play you've seen live!

- [ ] 278. *Dinner with Friends*, by Donald Margulies (2000)
- [ ] 279. *Wit*, by Margaret Edson (1999)
- [ ] 280. *How I Learned to Drive*, by Paula Vogel (1998)
- [ ] 281. *Rent*, by Jonathan Larson (1996)
- [ ] 282. *The Young Man from Atlanta*, by Horton Foote (1995)
- [ ] 283. *Three Tall Women*, by Edward Albee (1994)
- [ ] 284. *Angels in America*, by Tony Kushner (1993)
- [ ] 285. *The Kentucky Cycle*, by Robert Schenkkan (1992)
- [ ] 286. *Lost in Yonkers*, by Neil Simon (1991)
- [ ] 287. *The Piano Lesson*, by August Wilson (1990)
- [ ] 288. *The Heidi Chronicles*, by Wendy Wasserstein (1989)
- [ ] 289. *Driving Miss Daisy*, by Alfred Uhry (1988)
- [ ] 290. *Fences*, by August Wilson (1987)
- [ ] 291. *Sunday in the Park with George*, Sondheim & Lapine (85)
- [ ] 292. *Glengarry Glen Ross*, by David Mamet (1984)
- [ ] 293. *'Night, Mother*, by Marsha Norman (1983)
- [ ] 294. *A Soldier's Play*, by Charles Fuller (1982)
- [ ] 295. *Crimes of the Heart*, by Beth Henley (1981)
- [ ] 296. *Talley's Folly*, by Lanford Wilson (1980)

- [ ] 297. *Buried Child*, by Sam Shepard (1979)
- [ ] 298. *The Gin Game*, by Donald L. Coburn (1978)
- [ ] 299. *The Shadow Box*, by Michael Cristofer (1977)
- [ ] 300. *A Chorus Line*, Kirkwood, Jr.,Hamlisch,Dante,Kleban (1976)
- [ ] 301. *Seascape*, by Edward Albee (1975)
- [ ] 302. *That Championship Season*, by Jason Miller (1973)
- [ ] 303. *The Effect of Gamma Rays...*, by Paul Zindel (1971) *
- [ ] 304. *No Place to be Somebody*, by Charles Gordone (1970)
- [ ] 305. *The Great White Hope*, by Howard Sackler (1969)
- [ ] 306. *A Delicate Balance*, by Edward Albee (1967)
- [ ] 307. *The Subject Was Roses*, by Frank D. Gilroy (1965)
- [ ] 308. *How to Succeed in Business...*, Loesser & Burrows (1962) *
- [ ] 309. *All the Way Home*, by Tad Mosel (1961)
- [ ] 310. *Fiorello!*, by Weidman, Abbott, Bock and Harnick (1960)
- [ ] 311. *J. B.*, by Archibald Macleish (1959)
- [ ] 312. *Look Homeward, Angel*, by Ketti Frings (1958)
- [ ] 313. *Long Day's Journey Into Night*, by Eugene O'Neill (1957)
- [ ] 314. *Diary of Anne Frank*, by Hackett and Goodrich (1956)

* Give yourself a star for each play you've seen live!

- [ ] 315. *Cat on a Hot Tin Roof*, by Tennessee Williams (1955)
- [ ] 316. *The Teahouse of the August Moon*, by John Patrick (1954)
- [ ] 317. *Picnic*, by William Inge (1953)
- [ ] 318. *The Shrike*, by Joseph Kramm (1952)
- [ ] 319. *South Pacific*, by Rodgers, Hammerstein II & Logan (1950)
- [ ] 320. *Death of a Salesman*, by Arthur Miller (1949)
- [ ] 321. *A Streetcar Named Desire*, by Tennessee Williams (1948)
- [ ] 322. *State of the Union*, by Crouse and Lindsay (1946)
- [ ] 323. *Harvey*, by Mary Chase (1945)
- [ ] 324. *The Skin of Our Teeth*, by Thornton Wilder (1943)
- [ ] 325. *There Shall Be No Night*, by Robert E. Sherwood (1941)
- [ ] 326. *The Time of Your Life*, by William Saroyan (1940)
- [ ] 327. *Abe Lincoln in Illinois*, by Robert E. Sherwood (1939)
- [ ] 328. *Our Town*, by Thornton Wilder (1938)
- [ ] 329. *You Can't Take It With You*, by Hart and Kaufman (1937)
- [ ] 330. *Idiot's Delight*, by Robert E. Sherwood (1936)
- [ ] 331. *The Old Maid*, by Zoe Akins (1935)
- [ ] 332. *Men in White*, by Sidney Kingsley (1934)

- [ ] 333. *Both Your Houses*, by Maxwell Anderson (1933)
- [ ] 334. *Of Thee I Sing*, by Kaufman, Ryskind & Gershwin (1932)
- [ ] 335. *Alison's House*, by Susan Glaspell (1931)
- [ ] 336. *The Green Pastures*, by Marc Connelly (1930)
- [ ] 337. *Street Scene*, by Elmer L. Rice (1929)
- [ ] 338. *Strange Interlude*, by Eugene O'Neill (1928)
- [ ] 339. *In Abraham's Bosom*, by Paul Green (1927)
- [ ] 340. *Craig's Wife*, by George Kelly (1926)
- [ ] 341. *They Knew What They Wanted*, by Sidney Howard (1925)
- [ ] 342. *Hell-Bent Fer Heaven*, by Hatcher Hughes (1924)
- [ ] 343. *Icebound*, by Owen Davis (1923)
- [ ] 344. *Anna Christie*, by Eugene O'Neill (1922)
- [ ] 345. *Miss Lulu Bett*, by Zona Gale (1921)
- [ ] 346. *Beyond the Horizon*, by Eugene O'Neill (1920)
- [ ] 347. *Why Marry?* by Jesse Lynch Williams (1918)

* Give yourself a star for each play you've seen live!

READ

Shakespeare's Plays:

- [ ] 348. *A Midsummer Night's Dream*
- [ ] 349. *All's Well That Ends Well*
- [ ] 350. *Antony and Cleopatra*
- [ ] 351. *As You Like It*
- [ ] 352. *Coriolanus*
- [ ] 353. *Cymbeline*
- [ ] 354. *Hamlet*
- [ ] 355. *Henry IV, Part 1*
- [ ] 356. *Henry IV, Part 2*
- [ ] 357. *Henry V*
- [ ] 358. *Henry VI, Part 1*
- [ ] 359. *Henry VI, Part 2*
- [ ] 360. *Henry VI, Part 3*
- [ ] 361. *Henry VIII*
- [ ] 362. *Julius Caesar*
- [ ] 363. *King John*
- [ ] 364. *King Lear*
- [ ] 365. *Love's Labour's Lost*

- [ ] 366. *Macbeth*
- [ ] 367. *Measure for Measure*
- [ ] 368. *Much Ado About Nothing*
- [ ] 369. *Othello*
- [ ] 370. *Pericles, Prince of Tyre*
- [ ] 371. *Richard II*
- [ ] 372. *Richard III*
- [ ] 373. *Romeo and Juliet*
- [ ] 374. *The Comedy of Errors*
- [ ] 375. *The Merchant of Venice*
- [ ] 376. *The Merry Wives of Windsor*
- [ ] 377. *The Taming of the Shrew*
- [ ] 378. *The Tempest*
- [ ] 379. *The Two Gentlemen of Verona*
- [ ] 380. *The Winter's Tale*
- [ ] 381. *Timon of Athens*
- [ ] 382. *Titus Andronicus*
- [ ] 383. *Troilus and Cressida*
- [ ] 384. *Twelfth Night*

* Give yourself a star for each play you've seen live!

"**Helmer:** I would gladly work night and day for you, Nora - bear sorrow and want for your sake. But no man would sacrifice his honor for the one he loves.

Nora: It is a thing hundreds of thousands of women have done."

— Henrik Ibsen, A Doll's House

READ

the following plays:

- [ ] 385. *A Doll's House*, by Henrik Ibsen
- [ ] 386. *A Doll's House, Part 2*, by Lucas Hnath
- [ ] 387. *A Few Good Men*, by Aaron Sorkin
- [ ] 388. *A Man for All Seasons*, by Robert Bolt
- [ ] 389. *A Moon for the Misbegotten*, by Eugene O'Neill
- [ ] 390. *A Piece of My Heart*, by Shirley Lauro
- [ ] 391. *A Raisin in the Sun*, by Lorraine Hansberry
- [ ] 392. *A View from the Bridge*, by Arthur Miller
- [ ] 393. *A Woman of No Importance*, by Oscar Wilde
- [ ] 394. *After the Fall*, by Arthur Miller
- [ ] 395. *All in the Timing*, by David Ives
- [ ] 396. *All My Sons*, by Arthur Miller
- [ ] 397. *Almost, Maine*, by John Cariani
- [ ] 398. *Amadeus*, by Peter Shaffer
- [ ] 399. *American Buffalo*, by David Mamet
- [ ] 400. *An Enemy of the People*, by Henrik Ibsen
- [ ] 401. *An Ideal Husband*, by Oscar Wilde
- [ ] 402. *An Inspector Calls*, by J.B. Priestley

* Give yourself a star for each play you've seen live!

☐ 403. *Antigone*, by Sophocles

☐ 404. *Arcadia*, by Tom Stoppard

☐ 405. *Arms and the Man*, by George Bernard Shaw

☐ 406. *Arsenic and Old Lace*, by Joseph Kesselring

☐ 407. *Barefoot in the Park*, by Neil Simon

☐ 408. *Beyond Therapy*, by Christopher Durang

☐ 409. *Blasted*, by Sarah Kane

☐ 410. *Blithe Spirit*, by Noël Coward

☐ 411. *Blue Stockings*, by Jessica Swale

☐ 412. *Brighton Beach Memoirs*, by Neil Simon

☐ 413. *Circle Mirror Transformation*, by Annie Baker

☐ 414. *Cloud 9*, by Caryl Churchill

☐ 415. *Copenhagen*, by Michael Frayn

☐ 416. *Cyrano De Bergerac*, by Edmond Rostand

☐ 417. *Dancing at Lughnasa*, by Brian Friel

☐ 418. *Deathtrap*, by Ira Levin

☐ 419. *Desire Under the Elms*, by Eugene O'Neill

☐ 420. *Doctor Faustus*, by Christopher Marlowe

- [ ] 421. *Dog Sees God*, by Bert V. Royal
- [ ] 422. *Eclipsed*, by Danai Gurira
- [ ] 423. *Electra*, by Sophocles
- [ ] 424. *Endgame*, by Samuel Beckett
- [ ] 425. *Equus*, by Peter Shaffer
- [ ] 426. *Eurydice*, by Sarah Ruhl
- [ ] 427. *Faust*, by Johann Wolfgang von Goethe
- [ ] 428. *Five Women Wearing the Same Dress*, by Alan Ball
- [ ] 429. *For Colored Girls Who Have Considered Suicide...*, Shange *
- [ ] 430. *Fuddy Meers*, by David Lindsay-Abaire
- [ ] 431. *Ghosts*, by Henrik Ibsen
- [ ] 432. *God's Ear*, by Jenny Schwartz
- [ ] 433. *Green Grow the Lilacs*, by Lynn Riggs
- [ ] 434. *Happy Days*, by Samuel Beckett
- [ ] 435. *Harry Potter & the Cursed Child*, Tiffany, Thorne, Rowling
- [ ] 436. *Hedda Gabler*, by Henrik Ibsen
- [ ] 437. *Hir*, by Taylor Mac
- [ ] 438. *Incarnations*, by Clive Barker

* Give yourself a star for each play you've seen live!

☐ 439. *Inherit the Wind*, by Jerome Lawrence

☐ 440. *Intimate Apparel*, by Lynn Nottage

☐ 441. *Iphigenia in Aulis*, by Euripides

☐ 442. *Jitney*, by August Wilson

☐ 443. *Joe Turner's Come and Gone*, by August Wilson

☐ 444. *Lady Windermere's Fan*, by Oscar Wilde

☐ 445. *Look Back in Anger*, by John Osborne

☐ 446. *Lysistrata*, by Aristophanes

☐ 447. *M. Butterfly*, by David Henry Hwang

☐ 448. *Ma Rainey's Black Bottom*, by August Wilson

☐ 449. *Machinal*, by Sophie Treadwell

☐ 450. *Marisol*, by José Rivera

☐ 451. *Medea*, by Euripides

☐ 452. *Middletown*, by Will Eno

☐ 453. *Miss Julie*, by August Strindberg

☐ 454. *Moon Over Buffalo*, by Ken Ludwig

☐ 455. *Mother Courage and Her Children*, by Bertolt Brecht

☐ 456. *Mourning Becomes Electra*, by Eugene O'Neill

☐ 457. *Mr. Burns, a Post-Electric Play*, by Anne Washburn

☐ 458. *Murder in the Cathedral*, by T.S. Eliot

☐ 459. *Nell Gwynn*, by Jessica Swale

☐ 460. *No Exit*, by Jean-Paul Sartre

☐ 461. *Noises Off*, by Michael Frayn

☐ 462. *Oedipus Rex*, by Sophocles

☐ 463. *Oleanna*, by David Mamet

☐ 464. *One Flew Over the Cuckoo's Nest*, by Dale Wasserman

☐ 465. *Peter and Alice*, by John Logan

☐ 466. *Picasso at the Lapin Agile*, by Steve Martin

☐ 467. *Private Lives*, by Noël Coward

☐ 468. *Prometheus Bound*, by Aeschylus

☐ 469. *Pygmalion*, by George Bernard Shaw

☐ 470. *Red Light Winter*, by Adam Rapp

☐ 471. *Red*, by John Logan

☐ 472. *Rhinoceros / The Chairs / The Lesson*, by Eugène Ionesco

☐ 473. *Rosencrantz and Guildenstern Are Dead*, by Tom Stoppard

☐ 474. *Saint Joan*, by George Bernard Shaw

* Give yourself a star for each play you've seen live!

"If only we could see in advance all the harm that can come from the good we think we are doing."

— Luigi Pirandello, Six Characters in Search of an Author

- [ ] 475. *She Kills Monsters*, by Qui Nguyen
- [ ] 476. *She Stoops to Conquer*, by Oliver Goldsmith
- [ ] 477. *Six Characters in Search of an Author*, by Luigi Pirandello
- [ ] 478. *Six Degrees of Separation*, by John Guare
- [ ] 479. *Spring's Awakening*, by Frank Wedekind
- [ ] 480. *Steel Magnolias*, by Robert Harling
- [ ] 481. *Stop Kiss*, by Diana Son
- [ ] 482. *Suddenly Last Summer*, by Tennessee Williams
- [ ] 483. *Summer and Smoke*, by Tennessee Williams
- [ ] 484. *Tartuffe*, by Molière
- [ ] 485. *The Bacchae*, by Euripides
- [ ] 486. *The Bald Soprano*, by Eugène Ionesco
- [ ] 487. *The Birthday Party*, by Harold Pinter
- [ ] 488. *The Boys Next Door*, by Tom Griffin
- [ ] 489. *The Caucasian Chalk Circle*, by Bertolt Brecht
- [ ] 490. *The Cherry Orchard*, by Anton Chekhov
- [ ] 491. *The Children's Hour*, by Lillian Hellman
- [ ] 492. *The Cripple of Inishmaan*, by Martin McDonagh

* Give yourself a star for each play you've seen live!

55

☐ 493. *The Crucible*, by Arthur Miller

☐ 494. *The Curious Incident of the Dog* ..., Stephens & Haddon *

☐ 495. *The Diviners*, by Jim Leonard

☐ 496. *The Duchess of Malfi*, by John Webster

☐ 497. *The Elephant Man*, by Bernard Pomerance

☐ 498. *The Game's Afoot*, by Ken Ludwig

☐ 499. *The Glass Menagerie*, by Tennessee Williams

☐ 500. *The Goat, or Who is Sylvia?* by Edward Albee

☐ 501. *The God of Carnage*, by Yasmina Reza

☐ 502. *The History Boys*, by Alan Bennett

☐ 503. *The Homecoming*, by Harold Pinter

☐ 504. *The House of Bernarda Alba*, by Federico García Lorca

☐ 505. *The Humans*, by Stephen Karam

☐ 506. *The Iceman Cometh*, by Eugene O'Neill

☐ 507. *The Importance of Being Earnest*, by Oscar Wilde

☐ 508. *The Laramie Project*, by Moisés Kaufman

☐ 509. *The Last Days of Judas Iscariot*, by Stephen Adly Guirgis

☐ 510. *The Lion in Winter*, by James Goldman

*See pg. 95

☐ 511. *The Little Foxes*, by Lillian Hellman

☐ 512. *The Maids*, by Jean Genet

☐ 513. *The Man Who Came to Dinner*, by Kaufman & Hart

☐ 514. *The Miracle Worker*, by William Gibson

☐ 515. *The Misanthrope*, by Molière

☐ 516. *The Mountaintop*, by Katori Hall

☐ 517. *The Mousetrap*, by Agatha Christie

☐ 518. *The Odd Couple*, by Neil Simon

☐ 519. *The Oresteia*, by Aeschylus

☐ 520. *The Pillowman*, by Martin McDonagh

☐ 521. *The Playboy of the Western World*, John Millington Synge

☐ 522. *The Rover*, by Aphra Behn

☐ 523. *The School for Scandal*, by Richard Brinsley Sheridan

☐ 524. *The Seagull*, by Anton Chekhov

☐ 525. *The Skriker*, by Caryl Churchill

☐ 526. *The Three Sisters*, by Anton Chekhov

☐ 527. *The Threepenny Opera*, by Bertolt Brecht

☐ 528. *The Trojan Women*, by Euripides

* Give yourself a star for each play you've seen live!

- [ ] 529. *The Vagina Monologues*, by Eve Ensler
- [ ] 530. *The Wolves*, by Sarah DeLappe
- [ ] 531. *The Zoo Story*, by Edward Albee
- [ ] 532. *Theophilus North*, by Thornton Wilder
- [ ] 533. *Top Girls*, by Caryl Churchill
- [ ] 534. *Torch Song Trilogy*, by Harvey Fierstein
- [ ] 535. *Travesties*, by Tom Stoppard
- [ ] 536. *Tribes*, by Nina Raine
- [ ] 537. *Trifles*, by Susan Glaspell
- [ ] 538. *True West*, by Sam Shepard
- [ ] 539. *Twelve Angry Men*, by Reginald Rose
- [ ] 540. *Twilight: Los Angeles, 1992*, by Anna Deavere Smith
- [ ] 541. *Ubu Roi*, by Alfred Jarry
- [ ] 542. *Uncle Vanya*, by Anton Chekhov
- [ ] 543. *Under Milk Wood*, by Dylan Thomas
- [ ] 544. *Venus in Fur*, by David Ives
- [ ] 545. *Waiting for Godot*, by Samuel Beckett
- [ ] 546. *Waiting for Lefty*, by Clifford Odets

☐ 547. *Who's Afraid of Virginia Woolf?* by Edward Albee
☐ 548. *Whose Life Is It Anyway?* by Brian Clark
☐ 549. *Yellow Face*, by David Henry Hwang
☐ 550. A play not mentioned _____
☐ 551. A play not mentioned _____
☐ 552. A play not mentioned _____
☐ 553. A play not mentioned _____
☐ 554. A play not mentioned _____
☐ 555. A play not mentioned _____
☐ 556. A play not mentioned _____
☐ 557. A play not mentioned _____
☐ 558. A play not mentioned _____
☐ 559. A play not mentioned _____

* Give yourself a star for each play you've seen live!

MUSICALS

to see

SEE

the following:

- [ ] 560. *1776*
- [ ] 561. *42nd Street*
- [ ] 562. *9 to 5*
- [ ] 563. *A Bronx Tale*
- [ ] 564. *A Chorus Line*
- [ ] 565. *A Christmas Carol*
- [ ] 566. *A Funny Thing Happened on the Way to the Forum*
- [ ] 567. *A Gentleman's Guide to Love and Murder*
- [ ] 568. *A Little Night Music*
- [ ] 569. *A Little Princess*
- [ ] 570. *A Year with Frog and Toad*
- [ ] 571. *Aida*
- [ ] 572. *Ain't Misbehavin'*
- [ ] 573. *Aladdin*
- [ ] 574. *All Shook Up*
- [ ] 575. *Allegro*
- [ ] 576. *Amélie*
- [ ] 577. *American Idiot*

- [ ] 578. *American Psycho*
- [ ] 579. *An American in Paris*
- [ ] 580. *Anastasia*
- [ ] 581. *Annie*
- [ ] 582. *Annie Get Your Gun*
- [ ] 583. *Anyone Can Whistle*
- [ ] 584. *Anything Goes*
- [ ] 585. *Applause*
- [ ] 586. *Assassins*
- [ ] 587. *Avenue Q*
- [ ] 588. *Bandstand*
- [ ] 589. *Bare*
- [ ] 590. *Barnum*
- [ ] 591. *Bat Boy*
- [ ] 592. *Bat Out of Hell*
- [ ] 593. *Be More Chill*
- [ ] 594. *Beautiful: The Carole King Musical*
- [ ] 595. *Beauty and the Beast*

* Give yourself a star for each cast recording you've listened to!

"What good is sitting alone in your room? Come hear the music play."

— Cabaret

☐ 596. *Big Fish*

☐ 597. *Big River*

☐ 598. *Big*

☐ 599. *Billy Elliot*

☐ 600. *Blood Brothers*

☐ 601. *Bonnie & Clyde*

☐ 602. *Brigadoon*

☐ 603. *Bright Star*

☐ 604. *Bring It On*

☐ 605. *Bye Bye Birdie*

☐ 606. *Cabaret*

☐ 607. *Calamity Jane*

☐ 608. *Camelot*

☐ 609. *Candide*

☐ 610. *Carmen Jones*

☐ 611. *Caroline, or Change*

☐ 612. *Carousel*

☐ 613. *Carrie*

* Give yourself a star for each cast recording you've listened to!

- [ ] 614. *Catch Me If You Can*
- [ ] 615. *Cats*
- [ ] 616. *Charlie and the Chocolate Factory*
- [ ] 617. *Chess*
- [ ] 618. *Chicago*
- [ ] 619. *Cinderella*
- [ ] 620. *City of Angels*
- [ ] 621. *Come from Away*
- [ ] 622. *Company*
- [ ] 623. *Contact*
- [ ] 624. *Crazy for You*
- [ ] 625. *Damn Yankees*
- [ ] 626. *Dear Evan Hansen*
- [ ] 627. *Dirty Rotten Scoundrels*
- [ ] 628. *Dogfight*
- [ ] 629. *Dreamgirls*
- [ ] 630. *Elf*
- [ ] 631. *Eugenius!*

☐ 632. *Everybody's Talking About Jamie*

☐ 633. *Evil Dead*

☐ 634. *Evita*

☐ 635. *Falsettos*

☐ 636. *Fame*

☐ 637. *Fiddler on the Roof*

☐ 638. *Finding Neverland*

☐ 639. *Finian's Rainbow*

☐ 640. *Fiorello!*

☐ 641. *First Date*

☐ 642. *Flower Drum Song*

☐ 643. *Follies*

☐ 644. *Footloose*

☐ 645. *Forever Plaid*

☐ 646. *Freaky Friday*

☐ 647. *Frozen*

☐ 648. *Fun Home*

☐ 649. *Funny Girl*

* Give yourself a star for each cast recording you've listened to!

- [ ] 650. *Ghost Quartet*
- [ ] 651. *Godspell*
- [ ] 652. *Grand Hotel*
- [ ] 653. *Grease*
- [ ] 654. *Groundhog Day*
- [ ] 655. *Guys and Dolls*
- [ ] 656. *Gypsy*
- [ ] 657. *Hadestown*
- [ ] 658. *Hair*
- [ ] 659. *Hairspray*
- [ ] 660. *Hallelujah, Baby!*
- [ ] 661. *Hamilton*
- [ ] 662. *Heathers*
- [ ] 663. *Hedwig and the Angry Inch*
- [ ] 664. *Hello, Dolly!*
- [ ] 665. *Honk!*
- [ ] 666. *How to Succeed in Business Without Really Trying*
- [ ] 667. *If/Then*

- [ ] 668. *In the Heights*
- [ ] 669. *Into the Woods*
- [ ] 670. *James and the Giant Peach*
- [ ] 671. *Jane Eyre*
- [ ] 672. *Jekyll & Hyde*
- [ ] 673. *Jersey Boys*
- [ ] 674. *Jesus Christ Superstar*
- [ ] 675. *John & Jen*
- [ ] 676. *Joseph and the Amazing Technicolor Dreamcoat*
- [ ] 677. *Junie B. Jones*
- [ ] 678. *Kinky Boots*
- [ ] 679. *Kismet*
- [ ] 680. *Kiss Me, Kate*
- [ ] 681. *Kiss of the Spider Woman*
- [ ] 682. *La Cage aux Folles*
- [ ] 683. *Legally Blonde*
- [ ] 684. *Les Misérables*
- [ ] 685. *Little Shop of Horrors*

* Give yourself a star for each cast recording you've listened to!

- [ ] 686. *Love Never Dies*
- [ ] 687. *Mamma Mia!*
- [ ] 688. *Man of La Mancha*
- [ ] 689. *Martin Guerre*
- [ ] 690. *Mary Poppins*
- [ ] 691. *Matilda*
- [ ] 692. *Me and My Girl*
- [ ] 693. *Mean Girls*
- [ ] 694. *Memphis*
- [ ] 695. *Merrily We Roll Along*
- [ ] 696. *Miss Saigon*
- [ ] 697. *Murder Ballad*
- [ ] 698. *My Fair Lady*
- [ ] 699. *Natasha, Pierre & the Great Comet of 1812*
- [ ] 700. *Newsies*
- [ ] 701. *Next to Normal*
- [ ] 702. *Nine*
- [ ] 703. *Oklahoma!*

- [ ] 704. *Oliver!*
- [ ] 705. *On The Town*
- [ ] 706. *Once*
- [ ] 707. *Once on This Island*
- [ ] 708. *Once Upon a Mattress*
- [ ] 709. *Ordinary Days*
- [ ] 710. *Our House*
- [ ] 711. *Pacific Overtures*
- [ ] 712. *Parade*
- [ ] 713. *Passion*
- [ ] 714. *Peter Pan*
- [ ] 715. *Pipe Dream*
- [ ] 716. *Pippin*
- [ ] 717. *Preludes*
- [ ] 718. *Pretty Woman*
- [ ] 719. *Ragtime*
- [ ] 720. *Raisin*
- [ ] 721. *Redhead*

* Give yourself a star for each cast recording you've listened to!

"Measure your life
in love."

— Rent

- [ ] 722. *Rent*
- [ ] 723. *Return to the Forbidden Planet*
- [ ] 724. *Road Show*
- [ ] 725. *Rock of Ages*
- [ ] 726. *School of Rock*
- [ ] 727. *Seussical*
- [ ] 728. *She Loves Me*
- [ ] 729. *Show Boat*
- [ ] 730. *Shrek*
- [ ] 731. *Singin' in the Rain*
- [ ] 732. *Something Rotten!*
- [ ] 733. *Songs for a New World*
- [ ] 734. *South Pacific*
- [ ] 735. *Spamalot*
- [ ] 736. *SpongeBob SquarePants*
- [ ] 737. *Spring Awakening*
- [ ] 738. *Starlight Express*
- [ ] 739. *State Fair*

* Give yourself a star for each cast recording you've listened to!

- [ ] 740. *Sunday in the Park with George*
- [ ] 741. *Sunny Afternoon*
- [ ] 742. *Sunset Boulevard*
- [ ] 743. *Sweeney Todd: The Demon Barber of Fleet Street*
- [ ] 744. *Sweet Charity*
- [ ] 745. *Tarzan*
- [ ] 746. *The 25th Annual Putnam County Spelling Bee*
- [ ] 747. *The Band's Visit*
- [ ] 748. *The Best Little Whorehouse in Texas*
- [ ] 749. *The Book of Mormon*
- [ ] 750. *The Bridges of Madison County*
- [ ] 751. *The Civil War*
- [ ] 752. *The Color Purple*
- [ ] 753. *The Drowsy Chaperone*
- [ ] 754. *The Frogs*
- [ ] 755. *The Full Monty*
- [ ] 756. *The Hunchback of Notre Dame*
- [ ] 757. *The King and I*

☐ 758. The Last Five Years

☐ 759. The Light in the Piazza

☐ 760. The Lion King

☐ 761. The Most Happy Fella

☐ 762. The Music Man

☐ 763. The Mystery of Edwin Drood

☐ 764. The Pajama Game

☐ 765. The Phantom of the Opera

☐ 766. The Pirates of Penzance

☐ 767. The Producers

☐ 768. The Rocky Horror Show

☐ 769. The Scarlet Pimpernel

☐ 770. The Secret Garden

☐ 771. The Sound of Music

☐ 772. The Wedding Singer

☐ 773. The Who's Tommy

☐ 774. The Will Rogers Follies

☐ 775. The Wiz

Give yourself a star for each cast recording you've listened to!

☐ 776. *The Wizard of Oz*

☐ 777. *Thoroughly Modern Millie*

☐ 778. *Tick, Tick...Boom!*

☐ 779. *Titanic*

☐ 780. *[title of show]*

☐ 781. *Top Hat*

☐ 782. *Tuck Everlasting*

☐ 783. *Two Gentlemen of Verona*

☐ 784. *Urinetown*

☐ 785. *Violet*

☐ 786. *Waitress*

☐ 787. *West Side Story*

☐ 788. *Wicked*

☐ 789. *Wonderful Town*

☐ 790. *Xanadu*

☐ 791. *Young Frankenstein*

☐ 792. *You're a Good Man, Charlie Brown*

☐ 793. *Zanna, Don't!*

- [ ] 794. *Zombie Prom*
- [ ] 795. *Zorba*
- [ ] 796. A musical not mentioned _____
- [ ] 797. A musical not mentioned _____
- [ ] 798. A musical not mentioned _____
- [ ] 799. A musical not mentioned _____
- [ ] 800. A musical not mentioned _____
- [ ] 801. A musical not mentioned _____
- [ ] 802. A musical not mentioned _____
- [ ] 803. A musical not mentioned _____
- [ ] 804. A musical not mentioned _____
- [ ] 805. A musical not mentioned _____

* Give yourself a star for each cast recording you've listened to!

WATCH

these musical movies

- [ ] 806. *42nd Street* (1933)
- [ ] 807. *A Chorus Line* (1985)
- [ ] 808. *A Hard Day's Night* (1964)
- [ ] 809. *A Night at the Opera* (1935)
- [ ] 810. *A Star is Born* (1954)
- [ ] 811. *A Star is Born* (2018)
- [ ] 812. *Across the Universe* (2007)
- [ ] 813. *All That Jazz* (1979)
- [ ] 814. *An American in Paris* (1951)
- [ ] 815. *Annie* (1982)
- [ ] 816. *Beauty and the Beast* (2017)
- [ ] 817. *Bugsy Malone* (1976)
- [ ] 818. *Bye Bye Birdie* (1963)
- [ ] 819. *Cabaret* (1972)
- [ ] 820. *Charlie and the Chocolate Factory* (2005)
- [ ] 821. *Chicago* (2002)
- [ ] 822. *Chi-Raq* (2015)
- [ ] 823. *Chitty Chitty Bang Bang* (1968)

☐ 824. *Dr. Horrible's Sing-Along Blog* (2008)

☐ 825. *Dreamgirls* (2006)

☐ 826. *Easter Parade* (1948)

☐ 827. *EMO the Musical* (2016)

☐ 828. *Enchanted* (2007)

☐ 829. *Fame* (1980)

☐ 830. *Fiddler on the Roof* (1971)

☐ 831. *French Cancan* (1954)

☐ 832. *Funny Face* (1957)

☐ 833. *Funny Girl* (1968)

☐ 834. *Gentlemen Prefer Blondes* (1953)

☐ 835. *Gigi* (1958)

☐ 836. *Godspell* (1973)

☐ 837. *Grease* (1978)

☐ 838. *Guys and Dolls* (1955)

☐ 839. *Gypsy* (1962)

☐ 840. *Gypsy* (1993)

☐ 841. *Hair* (1979)

- [ ] 842. *Hairspray* (1988)
- [ ] 843. *Hairspray* (2007)
- [ ] 844. *Hedwig and the Angry Inch* (2001)
- [ ] 845. *Help!* (1965)
- [ ] 846. *High School Musical* (2006)
- [ ] 847. *Into the Woods* (2014)
- [ ] 848. *La La Land* (2016)
- [ ] 849. *Les Misérables* (2012)
- [ ] 850. *Little Shop of Horrors* (1986)
- [ ] 851. *Mamma Mia!* (2008)
- [ ] 852. *Man of La Mancha* (1972)
- [ ] 853. *Mary Poppins* (1964)
- [ ] 854. *Mary Poppins Returns* (2018)
- [ ] 855. *Meet Me in St. Louis* (1944)
- [ ] 856. *Monty Python's The Meaning of Life* (1983)
- [ ] 857. *Moulin Rouge!* (2001)
- [ ] 858. *Muppets Most Wanted* (2014)
- [ ] 859. *My Fair Lady* (1964)

- [ ] 860. *Newsies* (1992)
- [ ] 861. *Nine* (2009)
- [ ] 862. *Oklahoma!* (1955)
- [ ] 863. *Oliver!* (1968)
- [ ] 864. *On the Town* (1949)
- [ ] 865. *Once* (2006)
- [ ] 866. *Pennies From Heaven* (1981)
- [ ] 867. *Phantom of the Paradise* (1974)
- [ ] 868. *Porgy and Bess* (1959)
- [ ] 869. *Rent* (2005)
- [ ] 870. *Royal Wedding* (1951)
- [ ] 871. *Seven Brides for Seven Brothers* (1954)
- [ ] 872. *Singin' in the Rain* (1952)
- [ ] 873. *Sunshine on Leith* (2013)
- [ ] 874. *Sweeney Todd: The Demon Barber of Fleet Street* (2007)
- [ ] 875. *Sweet Charity* (1969)
- [ ] 876. *Swing Time* (1936)
- [ ] 877. *The Blues Brothers* (1980)

- [ ] 878. *The Cocoanuts* (1929)
- [ ] 879. *The Court Jester* (1955)
- [ ] 880. *The King and I* (1956)
- [ ] 881. *The Last Five Years* (2014)
- [ ] 882. *The Lure* (2015)
- [ ] 883. *The Muppet Movie* (1979)
- [ ] 884. *The Muppets* (2011)
- [ ] 885. *The Phantom of the Opera* (2004)
- [ ] 886. *The Producers* (1967)
- [ ] 887. *The Producers* (2005)
- [ ] 888. *The Rocky Horror Picture Show* (1975)
- [ ] 889. *The Sapphires* (2012)
- [ ] 890. *The Sound of Music* (1965)
- [ ] 891. *The Umbrellas of Cherbourg* (1964)
- [ ] 892. *The Wizard of Oz* (1939)
- [ ] 893. *The Young Girls of Rochefort* (1967)
- [ ] 894. *Tommy* (1975)
- [ ] 895. *Top Hat* (1935)

☐ 896. *Topsy-Turvy* (1999)

☐ 897. *Victor/Victoria* (1982)

☐ 898. *Viva Las Vegas* (1964)

☐ 899. *West Side Story* (1961)

☐ 900. *White Christmas* (1954)

☐ 901. *Willy Wonka and the Chocolate Factory* (1971)

☐ 902. *Yankee Doodle Dandy* (1942)

If you have any other favorite musical movies, list them here:

# EVERYTHING
else

85

WATCH THESE

theatre-related movies

- [ ] 903. *A Double Life* (1947)
- [ ] 904. *A Story of Floating Weeds* (1934)
- [ ] 905. *After the Rehearsal* (1984)
- [ ] 906. *All About Eve* (1950)
- [ ] 907. *An Actor's Revenge* (1963)
- [ ] 908. *Babes on Broadway* (1941)
- [ ] 909. *Being Julia* (2004)
- [ ] 910. *Birdman* (2014)
- [ ] 911. *Bullets Over Broadway* (1994)
- [ ] 912. *Caesar Must Die* (2012)
- [ ] 913. *Career* (1959)
- [ ] 914. *Children of Paradise* (1945)
- [ ] 915. *Henry V* (1989)
- [ ] 916. *Limelight* (1952)
- [ ] 917. *Looking for Richard* (1996)
- [ ] 918. *Me and Orson Welles* (2008)
- [ ] 919. *Moon Over Broadway* (1997)
- [ ] 920. *Mrs. Henderson Presents* (2005)

☐ 921. *Noises Off* (1992)

☐ 922. *Opening Night* (2016)

☐ 923. *Romeo + Juliet* (1996)

☐ 924. *Shakespeare in Love* (1998)

☐ 925. *Stage Fright* (1950)

☐ 926. *The Band Wagon* (1953)

☐ 927. *The Boy Friend* (1971)

☐ 928. *The Dresser* (1983)

☐ 929. *The Great Ziegfeld* (1936)

☐ 930. *The Last Metro* (1980)

☐ 931. *The Phantom of the Opera* (1925)

☐ 932. *Theatre of Blood* (1973)

☐ 933. *To Be or Not To Be* (1942)

☐ 934. *Twentieth Century* (1934)

☐ 935. *Vanya on 42nd Street* (1994)

If you have any other favorite theatre movies, list them here:

READ
the following books:

- [ ] 936. *A Challenge for the Actor*, by Uta Hagen
- [ ] 937. *A Director Prepares*, by Anne Bogart
- [ ] 938. *Acting as a Business*, by Brian O'Neil
- [ ] 939. *Acting Power*, by Robert Cohen
- [ ] 940. *Acting: The First Six Lessons*, by Richard Boleslavsky
- [ ] 941. *Actions*, by Marina Calderone
- [ ] 942. *Alexander Hamilton*, by Ron Chernow *
- [ ] 943. *An Actor Prepares*, by Constantin Stanislavsky
- [ ] 944. *Audition*, by Michael Shurtleff
- [ ] 945. *Changed for Good*, by Stacy Wolf
- [ ] 946. *Failing Up*, by Leslie Odom Jr.
- [ ] 947. *Freeing the Natural Voice*, by Kristin Linklater
- [ ] 948. *Finishing the Hat Set*, by Stephen Sondheim
- [ ] 949. *Impro*, by Keith Johnstone
- [ ] 950. *Improvisation for the Theatre*, by Viola Spolin
- [ ] 951. *Les Misérables*, by Victor Hugo *
- [ ] 952. *Letters to a Young Artist*, by Anna Deavere Smith
- [ ] 953. *Life Is Like a Musical*, by Tim Federle

- [ ] 954. *Mary Poppins*, by P.L. Travers *
- [ ] 955. *Not Since Carrie*, by Ken Mandelbaum
- [ ] 956. *Old Possum's Book of Practical Cats*, by T.S. Eliot *
- [ ] 957. *Oliver Twist*, by Charles Dickens *
- [ ] 958. *Original Story*, by Arthur Laurents
- [ ] 959. *Razzle Dazzle*, by Michael Riedel
- [ ] 960. *Respect for Acting*, by Uta Hagen
- [ ] 961. *Sanford Meisner on Acting*, by Sanford Meisner
- [ ] 962. *Shakespeare Saved My Life*, by Laura Bates
- [ ] 963. *Theatre of the Unimpressed*, by Jordan Tannahill
- [ ] 964. *The Actor and the Target*, Declan Donnellan
- [ ] 965. *The Actor's Life*, by Jenna Fischer
- [ ] 966. *The Archive and the Repertoire*, by Diana Taylor
- [ ] 967. *The Empty Space*, by Peter Brook
- [ ] 968. *The Secret Life of the American Musical*, Jack Viertel
- [ ] 969. *The Viewpoints Book*, *by* Anne Bogart & Tina Landau
- [ ] 970. *The Wonderful Wizard of Oz*, by L. Frank Baum *
- [ ] 971. *Towards a Poor Theatre*, by Jerzy Grotowski

☐ 972. *Tuck Everlasting*, by Natalie Babbitt *

☐ 973. *Up in the Cheap Seats*, by Ron Fassler

☐ 974. *War and Peace*, by Leo Tolstoy *

☐ 975. *What if It's Us*, by Becky Albertalli and Adam Silvera

☐ 976. *Wicked*, by Gregory Maguire *

List any other favorite theatre-related books here:

WATCH

these TV shows:

- [ ] 977. *Crazy Ex-Girlfriend*
- [ ] 978. *Empire*
- [ ] 979. *Encore!*
- [ ] 980. *Flight of the Conchords*
- [ ] 981. *Galavant*
- [ ] 982. *Glee*
- [ ] 983. *Modern Family* *
- [ ] 984. *Nashville*
- [ ] 985. *Slings & Arrows*
- [ ] 986. *Smash*
- [ ] 987. *Star*
- [ ] 988. *Submissions Only*
- [ ] 989. *Summer Heights High*
- [ ] 990. *The Kitchen Musical*
- [ ] 991. *Unbreakable Kimmy Schmidt*

* See pg. 95

WATCH

these documentaries:

☐ 992. *Best Worst Thing That Ever Could Have Happened*

☐ 993. *Every Little Step*

☐ 994. *Hamilton: One Shot to Broadway*

☐ 995. *Janey Makes a Play*

☐ 996. *Leonard Soloway's Broadway*

☐ 997. *Life After Tomorrow*

☐ 998. *McKellen Playing the Part*

☐ 999. *ShowBusiness: The Road to Broadway*

☐ 1000. *Six by Sondheim*

☐ 1001. *The Heat is Back On*

List any other favorite theatre documentaries here:

"I regard the theatre as the greatest of all art forms, the most immediate way in which a human being can share with another the sense of what it is to be a human being."

— Oscar Wilde

NOTES:

There are thousands of other plays, books, movies, musicals, and other stagey things that could have easily been included in this list. But this stuff is subjective! And that's why I've left lots of blank spaces for you to insert your own ideas.

And if you're wondering why any of the * items are marked:

Ellen's Stardust Diner - 50s-themed diner with singing waitstaff

Joe Allen - Regularly attracts Broadway patrons and actors

One Shubert Alley - Broadway-themed gift shop

Holy Trinity Church - Shakespeare's baptism site/church

The Effect of Gamma Rays on Man-in-the-Moon Marigolds (full title)

How to Succeed in Business Without Really Trying (full title)

For Colored Girls Who Have Considered Suicide / When the Rainbow Is Enuf, by Ntozake Shange (full title)

The Curious Incident of the Dog in the Night-Time (full title)

All the Starred Books - Books that later inspired musicals

Modern Family - So many theatre references - you'll love it!

P.S. In case you missed it at the beginning, make sure to check out www.stacykaryn.com/the-thespians-bucket-list for some freebies!

CREATE

your own bucket list

☐ 1.

☐ 2.

☐ 3.

☐ 4.

☐ 5.

☐ 6.

☐ 7.

☐ 8.

☐ 9.

☐ 10.

☐ 11.

☐ 12.

☐ 13.

☐ 14.

☐ 15.

☐ 16.

☐ 17.

☐ 18.

☐ 19.

☐ 20.

☐ 21.

☐ 22.

☐ 23.

☐ 24.

☐ 25.

☐ 26.

☐ 27.

☐ 28.

☐ 29.

☐ 30.

☐ 31.

☐ 32.

☐ 33.

☐ 34.

☐ 35.

☐ 36.

☐ 37.

☐ 38.

☐ 39.

☐ 40.

ABOUT
the author

Stacy Karyn is the founder of Theatre Trip, a published author, and a passionate theatrical entrepreneur. She has a TESOL drama certificate, a theatre degree from Hunter College in NYC, and has worked and interned with Broadway and Off-Broadway theatres.

Stacy has held theatre workshops in Hong Kong, Germany, The Netherlands, and Spain, all while enjoying theatrical performances around the world. All these experiences made her wish she had a theatre bucket list to physically interact with... so she made one that we can all enjoy!

Made in the USA
Middletown, DE
07 December 2020

26558688R00061